salmonpoetry

Diverse Voices from Ireland and the World

Navigating the Reach

MARY BUCHINGER

Published in 2023 by
Salmon Poetry
Cliffs of Moher, County Clare, Ireland
Website: www.salmonpoetry.com
Email: info@salmonpoetry.com

ISBN 978-1-915022-34-9

Cover Image: *Stephen Bodwell*
Cover Design & Typesetting: *Siobhán Hutson Jeanotte*

Printed in Ireland by Sprint Print

Dedicated with love to my parents

o

What is so rare as a day in June?
Then, if ever, come perfect days
JAMES RUSSELL LOWELL

Contents

i.

ii.

iii.

iv.

v.

vi.

                                                    Strange,
to see all that was once relation so loosely fluttering
hither and thither in space.

                              o

Once for each thing. Just once; no more. And we too,
just once. And never again. But to have been
this once, completely, even if only once:
to have been at one with the earth, seems beyond undoing.

                         —RAINER MARIA RILKE, *Duino Elegies*

i

At Mt. Auburn Cemetery

Sundays I walk across acres of the dead.
Grey tombs arch like eyelids.

Stone angels loom from pedestals,
wings weathering to sharpened nibs.

Blue jays quiz the air, insistent,
forage acorns, cache their goods.

A hawk's shriek ricochets overhead
and sometimes I feel hunted.

The Hawthorn Speaks

symmetry doesn't beckon the
eye   no—   disruption &
disorder   a lopsidedness that
reminds you   you are
dreaming the   rest of your
life asleep in   expectation
until a flat   smoothness
empty of bark   a swirl
& a swelling   around a
gap   the surface
wavy like   old   glass   the
slow assemblage   rippling
up the roughened   river

Dementia Diary #14

A gusty wind blows snow
from the east, from the north
then again from the east.
The snow is confused, my father says,
(beat) *sometimes we are too.*

Where better to look for the self
than in that snow, wind's prey,
swirling, resting for a moment
on the narrow elbow of a maple
before it's found out, whisked
away in a wispy puff toward
a locked-arm stand of firs.

Yesterday he looked out
on dirty banks of brittle ice
melting along the roadside
and said, *Last call for winter.*
Today, *oooing* over whiteouts,
he wonders what month we're in,
what, this window's strange offering.

In Flight Detroit - Boston

One goodbye after another   before
death   there is the dying   the sky in the
treble-paned window beside me beckons
Look   yellow bangle in a blue   dilating
triangle *Look* grainy grey light   how
long   how everlasting   the leaving of
home   a pyramid of pink lays itself down
on shadow-roughed dun   *Look* a light-
crazed cloud calls to me zigzag-light bats
batters our   wing   *mmump*   *mmump*
embroidered blue wave swells   dense
turbulence

furred chiffon
shimmery light   slips in   gives way to sheer
sundog   violet   green   gold-flocked
whispers *Move the self thus* (I take notes
I ask questions) Cloud   what is your light?
light loaned and magnified

deep
Prussian blue striped   eggshell blue watery
see-through keyhole cloud   I spy a silver
sister   a pink-curl contrail I too am part of
a parade of planes on a late afternoon   this
labor to locate the world of the self within
the larger   while   the light moves and I
move and

what's left
behind   straggles   dim dustbin lastness
clings   as the maroon sky's ocean rolls
over into navy flannel folds   grey
abandoned   dispersal of particle and wave
and now   this no-holds-barred dark   and
soon   too soon land again

Dying takes every day

asks everything
what you didn't even know was there
pulled from your very ends of being

I felt this when a stranger
passed me on the sidewalk
then broke into song—

contralto escaping
like a pent-up animal—
notes suddenly free

o

Every morning workers file
into the call center on Mass. Ave.

No matter what   they must dial
and speak   Almost no one
wants to talk with them

They are voices paid
to read scripts

Only on breaks—
cigarette   snack—
can they say what they want

o

I know a thread inside
is unspooling
will one day come up short—

but Thursday rolls round again
lunch dinner sleep

it's June the basil leaves
broaden
soon the solstice—

all its inordinate light

Fetch she says

                tossing
a long ungainly stick
to her golden retriever

I watch as the dog
bounds full of intention
it pounces   then sinks
its teeth into the bark

paws curl around
one crooked end
the dog settles in
to chomp the stick
bit by bit by bit
to a stubborn nub—

Fall's slant sun catches
in the dog's wispy fur
lingers in the leaves
that dangle their gold

and I want to climb
inside the tent of light
Stay me here Stay Stay

Evacuate

dream blankets bed mug chair slippers shower stairs house
sidewalk train bridge path hall faucet desk teapot classroom
tongue lung lunchbox office pencil bus book brain daylong day

ii

Roots

Most come from my mother's early summer garden, some from the gardens of her sisters— yarrow, chocolate mint—some from the old farm—peonies, dahlias, cannas. A hardy cactus—crown of hairy spears—spaded out from my cousin's yard. We load the damp, dirt-thick roots into the car, head East.

No question what to do the first day we're back—my son and I ready the front yard: compost, mulch. Dig holes, fill them with water; my hands remember wet soil. We place plants according to height, eventual bulk, their relation to fences. All but the bleeding hearts take.

August drought, the house sinks, foundation walls crack. When the contractor comes he sees only the fence— would you like us to put it back when we finish? Not a word about the plants. Warm, sunny weekends pass.

November and the last chance before deep frost, I put on my wool coat, dig into the same soft peat that's betraying the house, rip the carpet of violets, hit rogue raspberry roots—again that smell of wet soil. I carry the plants with my shovel to the row of new holes. My son tamps down the dirt. This is place-holder planting, temporary for winter, but how could they know.

Late March and the River's Numb

Leaden grey ice here
and there, a running dark
open beneath the bridge.

Tangled black tights
and a knotted scarf suture
two floating fragments.

An empty fifth of bourbon bobs—
someone's anesthesia.

A bag of clementines
plasters itself   wet, bright
against a small grimy floe.

The morning sky laden with spring rain
readies to wake the patient.

Bound

The man walking this path
   in the city fens listens too
      to the morning geese and jays

         In a torn jacket
and filthy chinos he's steady
on his feet

     I watch him study reflections
of reeds in the stream
  edged by rock and trash

        His gaze turns
toward the tree I love the old cherry
  with a gaping hole in its trunk—

        a dead part of itself
  it has found a way around—

  what remains
leans into the north wind

sap upsurges
     into its spring buds—

          coiled nubs
like new wounds on the limbs
  light-seeking

More from the trees:

After their leaves let go
limbs reveal the essential

grace of being
one with many parts

each responding to its portion
of light and rain

o

Branches thicken
as they grow

they crisscross
trajectories intersect

contact opens
each to the other

rupture
    becomes
        embrace

the membrane
cloaks the distance

limb and limb
draw into one

o

Growth is movement
away from a center

a testing and bridging
of emptiness

by unseen roots
spread wide   anchored deep

o

Even with a gap
in the heart of a trunk

it's possible to continue
to lengthen outward

response to damage an endless
investment and compromise

a hollow may serve as passage
and rot a perfect dwelling

o

Impervious and silent
are not what they seem

the bark is nothing but scars—

stretched runneled
trenched beetled apart

Big, with Rift

Outdoor art installation by Steven Siegel
DeCordova Museum, Lincoln, Massachusetts

In an abandoned stone foundation
tall stacks of folded newspapers

like exposed middens
slump toward each other

Rain and snow soften
the thousand edges

chipmunks tunnel beneath
sun-burnt headlines

late fall tendrils of flora
trail the margins

The rift narrows with time
the blue-black news washed grey

stories once urgent and lively
secreted inside tucked away

Sometimes wonder—

after Marianne Boruch

an inked sky its few
　　thousand throwaway stars

　must have been Michigan
　　　a coppery of airs

will I find another?

an acre out of that field
our kind inheritance rare
good farmland

　we toiled until something
was freed   practically

rows   plantings   a great
undertaking   not just
bare-bones necessary

and oh the fossils!
creatures and corals
bundled in limestone

　rounded by rain
and broken
　beneath the eave
of the rag-grey barn

my now and again heaven

　whole dark speech
a testament that wanders

Dear one—

Here is the world I leave you
no hope

flood   ebb
beauty   pain   beauty

you will feast with flies
then be their feast

every day's teacup
leaves its leavings

of these dregs   child
something make

iii

Dementia Diary #5

On the descent toward the small airport,
I know my parents wait for me
and that when we turn toward home,
my father will again point out the place
a plane crashed decades ago.

I remember my high school gym teacher
couldn't stop talking about it, how he picked up
body parts, books, shoes, purses, all that luggage
split open, vials, perfumes, pills, pajamas
sprawled on wet grass, but not his job
to sort things out, he was just a volunteer.

When I land, I will be daughter once more,
my father, astonished, happy to see me.
Right there, he'll say, *a plane went down. A plane
went down. Right there. A plane. There.*

Dementia Diary #16

I'm home for a short visit
in the middle of a mid-summer drought.

Then the sky closes its usual eye and
rainwater bounces off the hard dirt.

What is wanted
is something long, lingering.

My father picks up the newspaper.
He reads the headline: *Pre-Prom Shooting*.

I was crawling away, my best friend was shot, blood all over.

He looks up at me and asks,
Why do they want to shoot each other?

(Beat.)

Pre-Prom Shooting. I was crawling away,
my best friend was shot, blood all over.

He asks, *Can you imagine?*

Pre-Prom Shooting, he reads.
I was crawling away.

(Beat.)

Pre-Prom Shooting,

I hide the paper.

And now more rain.

It settles the day,
soaks the deep-dry grass.

Killdeer

Indian camps lingered in pockets
of thinned Michigan woods
long after a treaty took millions
of acres and moved the nations
Chippewa Ottawa Potawatomi
far beyond the blue necklace
of the sacred Lakes

Indian Dave—*Ish-don-quit*—
Crossing Cloud—son of a chief
lived old-style in Tuscola County
   he baked clay-covered fish
and snare-trapped game

   stayed even after
his first family was taken
by smallpox

He stayed trading
homemade baskets
hickory whip-stalks
   and gun-wipers

A gunnysack of ginseng on his back
he'd brandish a tomahawk in town parades
   to delight the crowds

His son James signed as if mute
   with the white people
spoke Algonquian with his father

and always followed behind
   as they walked the road
            a narrow ancestral trail
            drumming within

o

One day Margaretha was left
alone at home with the kitchen full
of fresh homemade bread—
    the morning's labor—
while her mother Anna
walked to town to get more flour

Protect the bread from the Indians
    Anna ordered
We need the money from the trainmen!

The daughter was twelve
like I was twelve
when I first remember
my mother telling me
her grandmother's story

No one now knows
if the Indians threatened Margaretha
or how many there were
They appeared at the door
lured by the aroma

When Anna returned and
found the bread gone
she chased her daughter
with a knife they said
    a long butcher knife

chased her for miles and miles
till she gave up finally
and Margaretha sheltered
ever after at her uncle's house
beside the tavern

Never again did
she go home

Anna filed for divorce
  a first in the county
and sold the farm
    it was hers to sell

She married the town doctor
and I believe he loved
fierce Anna's bread
and paid and paid
for each loaf after

o

On the homestead   Matthias and Emma
three and five years old   sent to fetch
the cows from the back forty

picked their way through twisty woods
and fields of stumps rough-cut
burnt   some half-dragged-out   roots
grasping at bare ankles bare feet

brother and sister
hand-in-hand as in a fairy tale
leading the cows back to the barn before dark

Ma stood outside the chinked-log cabin
to call them in   the children the cows
bells jangling   more than ninety years ago

My grandfather tells the story from his easy chair
his white-haired head sinking toward his chest
a lit cigar trembles between his elegant gnarled fingers

He remembers how his legs had ached
how tired he got fetching the cows
Steh auf! his sister would say

pulling him to his feet
He wonders how they didn't get lost

Emma now a hundred years old
with a long nose matching his own
their skin speckled translucent

She still pulls the dandelions
from her front yard in town
Can't bear to see something grow
where it don't belong

o

On the first warm days at the farm
my father pulled a spring-toothed
harrow with the John Deere
in the flat brown field leveling the tilth
readying readying and I rode
beside him balanced on the green
fender above the giant tire
fat-tracked tread spinning
below me all the colors of earth
grey black yellow red

throttle opened wide
we'd piece the field
half to quarter to eighths
round and round slowing only
at each turn *putt putt putt*
by the mucky clay-hipped
ditches cut by shiny culverts

I loved the air and thrum   this manly
puttering along drumming of dirt
in the sun in the wind   aye la hum
in the sun in the wind   aye la hum la hum

Flocks of glaucous seagulls
from Saginaw Bay followed like chaos
close behind swooping down
to feast on the newly-bared grubs
their *keow mew mew ha-ha-ha*
rising above the metal tine
clatter and galloping carburetor

o

Though it was my job
my father usually spotted her first
her awkward dance   wing held
out from her small body
that pod of hollow bones

kill-deer! kill-deer! she cried
as she floundered just in front
of the gyrating tractor tires
where cold-shoveled clods
of rough-waved dirt and stubble
waited for us to come break them
into workable ground
somewhere there   her nest

Almost always the killdeer's
broken-wing ruse worked
to save her pebbled cradle of eggs

Engine cut my father and I would jump
down from the tractor hunt the grey-
brown field for her grey-brown cluster—
  one time less than a feather away
from the dual front tires—
  what crushing we were capable of!

My father would stake the nest
with a white handkerchief flag
and the spring planting would obey—
a zig of the drill that dropped the seeds
left a comma in the summer-fat field
long after the fledglings had flown away

o

How straight the rows now

Those who farm that same flat land
ride in air-conditioned plexiglass boxes
wireless headphones cancel the noise

An earth-circulating satellite directs
the enormous tractor's course
no killdeer nests on the GPS

Loud gulls still follow behind still dive

Dementia Diary #34

Thank God for chickadees—
busybodies at the feeder—
for their brief flights
and black-capped banter
wassailing the air
a jubi-jubi-lee of *fee-bee-bee*

for the rascally squirrel
chivvying the winter birds
it leaps and misses barely
the heaped-up cage of seeds
Oh! we gasp *Oh!*

and we give thanks
for the three deer their ease
as they rove the skirt of woods
stepping out from dun-colored trees
to criss-cross old snowy trails
like a thought of—
a thought of a thought

No way but

in   no in but   out   the trap
tightens its teeth at every shift   a clench
just eat the green   gorge on green
there is no best branch   black grackle at my feet
three dry grasslets stiff straws in your beak
and yet you pick up a fourth without losing
what you have   who would have imagined
another spring   another go round   as one
hollows out   the other moves in   as one makes
light of light the other spreads thin *we* is
always under contention I mean construction
oh where did we put that cocoon?
                    And look a broom
broken   in the road bristles every which way
scattered singles needing to be swept incompetent
broom beneath the tire tread *Tired* reads
the memoryless man who cannot but read aloud
each word its sound and fury he gives voice
these straits that lead to straits *all straits
and none but straits* cosmographer come
oh map-maker make the map
that joins east with west
                    I spot two blue jays
loitering who ought to be busy building their nest
instead stock-still they look up at the man
sawing *wahaa!* branches of a tree   all three of us
watch   me with relief   they are only trimming
the tree   this white truck and neon-vested crew
only branch-picking today   for once not the whole-
hearted trunk cut wicked into us deeper   but the jays
so nervous and blue   maybe they had claimed one
of the branches now   no
                    going back no forward
say it in the teeth of the chainsaw   in the leaf
whose only traits were green and nutritious
say that you landed   my love   mine to catch

43

and I am nothing but green so eat all of me
one day I will fly out of here with you my Ticket
I name you Ticket though I brought you into this mess
shall we claim it what's been made is what awaits
you   your change   your charge no way in   but out
no out   but in

iv

Dementia Diary #22

A Life Drawing—

FATHER

I could be wrong

DAUGHTER

(My pencil—a scout, gathers information
    from the inside out
      trapezius to clavicle)

Would it be alright if I borrowed this book?

It's your book, Dad. It's okay.

Do you think they'd mind if I took it home?

You are home. This is where you live.

When will we go home?

(Drop a vertical line to push off from
Measure the angles
What o'clock is the drop of the deltoid?)

A farmer should know his land.

(The pencil, extension of my arm
The line on the page a symbol in space
    of space)

Did you marry a good farmer with a nice farm?

    (Follow the line, not the light and dark)

You're my second cousin, that's right.

    (Feet planted
    Sway like a willow)

I could be wrong.

    (I locate the pit of his neck nestled
    in his sternomastoid
    and then on my paper)

Hie, look at that bird in the maple!
Look at the squirrel!

    What's that bird want from the squirrel?

Look at them go!

    What a funny pair!

The winter wheat is greening up nice

    (but the line out there is swallowed
    in meaning—
    how can I uninterpret?)

You're leaving? Today? You're taking off?

(When I don't look so hard
the what's out there
to the side
drifts into my awareness)

Oh, I am so dumb.
A season and a season and a season
and a season—how many are there?

(What I discover when I close one eye)

Transit

suitcases roll   monorail red   blue back   forth
overhead   a sparrow   dodges   dives   wings
careen   indoors   beside   the   fountain   where
fractured water arcs across a black stone mirror
mirroring bird & birches & birch-white piano *Do
Not Touch* auto-playing Moonlight Sonata jazz
hands

              Concourse crossed B as in Boy
passenger sprinting last call calling at gate A
Alpha   now all passengers must   doors are
closing   Sky Chef rises truck extends   up & up
food in plastic   waste & water   wings &
whistles   *one would never expect death might
enter here*   we are born to tell how the ones
we love died   those we pray for   skin to skin

                        *Tug Tug
Push Back* printed on painted boxes on the
tarmac   O woman in the orange vest   you are
on now   hunched & hooded   you are reflective
& *on* in the city of little trucks that zip across
the oil-stained cement   bumping-almost into
neon green cone-sprouts   *Delta* means change
means convergence & effluvium what's left at
the going   a credit card special   free money
today   words cross in air   paging *Mister* &
what's allowed

                       flight's full
full cooperation required   please people   plane
tail-up perky   in line behind the surging others
our metal wings flex   windows *brum* come
go (wave) silence is not absence   exhaustion
speaks what's its timbre   tell me why his
death feels true like nothing else

                                    sheets of
transparent blue fall past the window   we
shadow toy ships on Huron's opaque ribbed
cloth & *Oh!* slender-hipped silos on the shore
toss nuclear smoke-rings across the great
turquoise lake wind-strewn steam hats renew &
renew   particles sifting down   the blast of
movement this up & outward sweep of self
along   will fall bit by bit   or all to bits
bellowed out   across land & lake   grey ash
and graphite spilling

Visits Home

Visit is to come and go. To arrive, then leave.
To be all of oneself in a place
and then to take that self away again.

o

As soon as I arrive, I am small. So familiar
these accents on my tongue, these smells in the kitchen.
Old appetites return, surprise me.

o

How can you visit what you can't leave.

Or leave what doesn't leave you.

o

I walk in the door and they hug me. Each time.
Each time two pies cooling on the counter.

o

My father takes hold of my hand,
squeezes my fingers, *Oh! You're home!*
Looks again to make sure.
Blinks, checks his hand for mine.

o

My bag is heavy and I struggle with it.
I am not me, whole swathes of myself missing
or turned invisible.
Who is it they hug?

o

My father and I visit. We come and go. I come, he leaves.
He visits the world, again, again, with wonder.
Oh, when did you get here? Hi!
Hello!

o

In my dream,
I sit in the soft saddle
of a sable brown rabbit
its broad shoulders hold me,
my hands clasp its tall, translucent ears,
sun streams through
as we fly through the air.

I wake to the day of leaving again.

o

Oh, this is where we were going? Bringing you here?
Holds my hand. *This is what we're doing now?*
A kiss. A hug. A kiss.
(please, no tears)

You're going away?

Opaque

Suspended between cities
I cross the bridge on foot

cars buses bikes rush by
muted in matte grey light

Yesterday someone jumped
into this icy river

I wonder where she stood
how she managed to die from here

which of my skyline beacons
did she last see

who saw her mid-air
who called

I a mile away maybe
mounting steps to work

or turning the key
in my door

Catastrophe

What were the signs when should
you have thought   something
might— what was missed   how
long the approach   a shadow
change in the air intake of breath

              the river in
the fens looks up says *I only see*
what I see   I show you everything
I can   bare trees   gnawed by
winter ragged ice-broke limbs leak
sap   an absence of clouds   a
feather drifts down   floats—

              mix of mud
and dirt-ice beside the bank
frozen boot tracks soften as the
ground gives up its cold   when
will the worms feel it is time how
will their churning change the
earth   what is in the works

              the upthaw
February sun strokes each green-
necked drake   equinox in sight
everything lengthening   opening
of wings and birdsong   early leaf-
buds lace river's mirror   see the
water breathe away from reeds

              city sirens reel in air   what
should a person—   where to
look? how? drum of helicopter
bus brakes sigh   someone   is
speeding *listen*   acceleration

can you only look back   *she was*
still smiling at that age   still an
easiness there   the place of
warning   what was missed   what
did you need to wish to have seen
to have known

                even now the lateness
of the hour the pastness of what
was   closing   the   ever-to-be
slipping into being   and not
attending to what?   you *pay pay*
pay before or after

                    you will never
know what seed fell from your
boot what did you carry   how to
catch on to the change before its
wake of disaster

                          quick
on furred feet when there's time
still   time   the   red-winged
blackbird   keeps calling *Okalee!*
My reed It's mine It's   mine
Okalee! My reed It's mine It's
mine

                    What o
what does the soft grey rabbit
know carried high up in a clutch
of claw?

Along The Fens

The river steps out from ice,
shivers its long throat
beside shoulders of old snow.

One wedge of white splits
the watery dark, lifts into a swan
alone trolling shallows.

Currents below,
currents above,
we are barely even here.

The guards at the museum door—
two ancient marble lions,
a shrug of green
troubling their manes—

grow more gaunt,
more fearsome
as their stone sugars down.

Tenshin-en / Garden of the Heart of Heaven

Museum of Fine Arts, Boston

broad leaves shelter stacked rocks
moss softens the verge

islands of boulders anchor the sun
pines drape the distance

water spills into a granite bowl
beside a bench that holds me

what suffers doesn't live here
whatever is brought is borne

greys and greens reveal
an endlessness

the procession of small stones
raked each morning

V

Waiting

Somewhere is the room
with people I love

a room with stiff chairs
the on and on
of my father's remaining work

My brother texts a picture—

our parents holding hands
freckled worn
made of my skin

bleached hospital sheet
thin gold rings

I imagine the hymns surrounding them

o

In my dream I find stones
pale and blue-veined
and eat them
one after another

A little boy crouches down beside me
Can you really eat those? he asks

Yes I say
smoothing a small stone with my fingers
sliding it into my mouth

The Meadow

after Mei-mei Berssenbrugge

Sunlight spirals out from a confusion
of tag alder that crowds the edges
of this narrow expanse

In the felt heat of the midday   dragonflies
swim in the light   splash in its waves

The sunk light begets   in the bed of me
exact frequencies of the meadow

The entire meadow—grasses dipped in gold—
spins like a rolled-open tunnel
my eyes sweep its sides fanning photonic fire

Behind me a small vernal pool
recedes in August death
a nerve of babyskin tadpoles
floats tardily in the thick brew

Innumerable opulent insects

Parting joe-pye weed
I wade through switchgrass
hope against arrival   the sun lacquers
my shoulders   freckles my hands

heat festers down to decay
and my spidery self emerges

o

In the miry pool   a branch springs
as its sunning turtle clambers off—

spectacle of plated light!—new
mud beneath its hooked green legs bubbles
bubbles I imagine against my skin

   skin—a thunderbolt of enzymes—
separates physical selves   frogs
turtles   me   what is felt

Do they too smell this dry juniper
I crush its thin gymnastic branches
between my fingers
release the gin of the waxy blue

I taste its air   wonder
what is essence   what can I
        do without   so chorded
so exacting my neediness
and hunger   nuclei buzz
all around me

                    o

I'm telling you the meadow
is a metaphor for dying

whereas   for the light
the dragonfly itself is keeper

                    o

The meadow opens its green mouth
and I am drawn to its activity
beauty and buzz

And yet   a rill of unease
courses between what I see
and what I know

between what I seek
and what I hold

The meadow explains this truth
I sit on a stone bridge and listen

o

The mudhole at my back jumps to life
with a quantity of dying   its troubled air
I inhale   invite inside

Here   with utter surrender   light
is sentient   this light in the skin of the meadow
complicated by a thousand daily things

Each blade sings

In these vibrations between meadow
and light   I plumb balance

o

phosphorescence   abundance   senescence

o

I aim for union with the meadow
and its light   how it opens and closes

its lessons absolute and consequential

Succession means
pioneers make way
for what's to come

   The alders and aspen will win this meadow
ready it for the oaks and beeches
to follow

Rocks will assemble without intent

The unbearable fervor of June
is the cost of August

Dragonfly   dragonfly

part or particle of God

What are the funeral rites
in this place

        where do the flowers
come from—no roadside chicory
    no wild carrot no timothy—

           airy palms
pinned with crimson carnations
  pungent cinnamon spice

    coverers of death not
in season not homegrown
but hailing from a sunny other realm

    and lily lily pale lily
floats above all   its milk
stamen-stained gold

      Who loves me best
and where now do I
belong   passed

from embrace to embrace
ready to be picked
and vased

      whole opposing
worlds lodge within me

Fishing at the dam after my father's funeral

I love nothing more
than to keep my eyes steady
on the red and white
of the tiny bobber

sky-blue water
beats against
its hollow body
an endless succession
of small-breath waves

Beneath—

  a cloaked hook

the worm
that wrapped my finger
with its dark purple earth
  now punctured
  helpless in the current

    barb buried inside

At the bonfire   a firefly

   gets tangled in my braid
light lighting up
strands of grey

One log collapses
into another a spindle
of sparks   still I
don't feel warm
inside this ring
of people
talking against
the shadows

        Someone heaves in
an old Adirondack chair—
ocean-salted wood
inhales flame   I
imagine sitting in it
fenced by fire
beneath the star-burnt sky

The stray intermittent light
  of the firefly
       blue ghost   still caught
   still traveling picks its way
   painstaking through my braid
calls me back

After a Storm

A giant pine rests against
the saplings gathered around it

its loosed limbs ooze sap
crushed needles scent the air

the roots jolted from the earth
release their grip on stones

the new-swept forest floor
fills with sun

(dream)

I have to clear the wet snow—
    a heavy weight

from the roof of our vehicle
    an unstable contraption

poised at the top of an incline
      only down to go

my father in front
    my arms around his chest

I hold on to him
and ease the brake

      ice slick in the dark
      I try to slow us stay
      in the track   keep us
      steady in this descent

vi

Prayer

time's interpreter
back stairway   window well
storm door   catch-all
borrowed light

Navigating the Reach

Off the coast of Maine
on remote Norton Island
a month after my father died
the moon has yet to practice
this particular loss

I've seen it quartered
like this before but this
inexorable waning after
blooming full   summer
solstice between
city buildings—

and I now islanded
beneath the naked spurs of stars

o

The tide comes round swollen
    then tattered in retreat

  in its wake   ropes—
braided and frayed
knotted to a hollow jug
or snaking empty

    ropes useless stranded
on rocks   the rocks   immovable
truths   complicate everything

    I watch my step
having learned through slipping
the slickness of the black algae
on the steep creviced granite

o

I'm told this is a reach
   and the island is joined
at low tide with another
by a gut—mucky crossing
for deer   sheep   mice

All day thrushes
here drop silver coins
into silver cups

   My father loved to whistle
ribboning the air   *abide*
with me   bicycle built for two
you make me happy
when skies are grey—

I watch a raccoon wash
its paws between boulders
   ocean shimmering beyond
its hunched shoulders   emerald
forest at its back   the kitchen
trash bags ransacked

o

My Michigan girl-dream
of a tide pool
I could not know—

   and now face to face
with the real thing the startling
ruddy and blue calico
the many many mouths
opening pops of seaweed
sea lice   barnacles—
Atlantic air   sun-thick
salt-damp

To sit like this and receive
receive   never would I
have dreamed this light-
lending inflorescence

How much we
can't foresee

Two translucent
dime-sized crabs scuttle
in a bottoming-out rivulet

A shadow-filled shrimp pushes
away with its army of legs

  One lone detached lobster claw

At dinner someone asks

  Was your father
   an extraordinary man?

  Extraordinary? I don't—
   don't know
        he was mine
      and I loved him

                    o

The trail through this mossy rock-
and clay-floored forest
is marked by buoys
impaled on broken limbs

  Half-buoys   trawler-bit buoys
glow orange and turquoise
suspended debris heart-height
as displaced as a childhood memory
of holding his hand   playing

with his ring the smell of his pipe
the cherry tobacco   Buoys
strangely guide me here
among trick traps of sadness

Still   sometimes   the deer—
   unseen except for their paths
of crushed and pawed moss—

tempt me to stray
to lay my cheek down
on the uneasy green

I say I have to get my bearings
 as if it's a matter
of walking a perimeter
   establishing direction
finding where the sun will sink

o

In an open cove
an eagle swoops down
like a broadhanded sorrow
     I shield myself
        heart pounding
     surprised by its immensity

At my feet I find
a smooth flat rock
that fits exactly
in my palm
  It is the shape
and heft of grief

I launch the rock out into the reach
it skips the surface three times
before it drops
below

Hours later when I return
to the flushed-out cove
a rock   mine?   sits shining
ringed in seaweed
wet   like something newly born
a rock on top of a rock
on top of a rock

o

In deep woods   wreckage
of mussels pried open plucked
  the pine needle path pocked
with scat of alabaster shells
purpled with urchin
what couldn't be digested

I inspect a lace of lichen
and out flutters a matching
must-colored moth   I
want oneness like this
or is it only camouflage?

A hermit crab scurries
from emptiness
into emptiness
and so on

Everywhere here   the blank
awful open eyes
of paper wasp nests
abandoned like silent
scraps of poetry

o

The island's held together
by spiders   the invisible
sticky portals they spin
their come-what-may:
hapless fly airy catkins
hemlock litter
awkward caterpillar
caught dangle here

On the eastern side a storm
blew through some years ago
now the grey knackered twists
of uprooted trees lean on
the green survivors
the living the dead entangled

o

Fog   a burgeoning hush
ushers in fishing boats

The island bows out
stage swept of detail

   Part of me remembers
everything is still here
nothing really has changed

My eyes keep returning
to the knobby dead birch
   a solid shape within
   the blunting grey

o

The island is part
of an archipelago
as everything is part of something
this island is one of three thousand
on the polka-dot coast
of jagged crags

How does one learn
to navigate the reach
    its treacherous rocks?

Some here call them stones
these things that could kill you
Others make them known
naming each one—See that?
Whale Rock   This one Snakehead
To these I add
Leviathan and Thief

One giant rock
    leavings of a wave or glacier
perches triangular on a shelf   looks seaward
Touchstone Rock—*it brings good luck*—
    Just touch it! So massive
I could live inside   gaze toward
Portugal   it's made of mirrors—
fractured quartz—my body
draped against the sun-saddled Rock
absorbs its warm fortune

o

Dusk   high tide
we climb into the boat
circle the island——spy
one stepped-rock outcrop
strung with white birds on stilts

beside them a larder of harbor seals
shatters suddenly into frenzied water
they disappear like a probed emotion
then surface   curious   observe us
with solemn fatherly eyes

o

Every island must have its snake
its bit of trouble even here
in this experiment of beauty

and when you think there could be
nothing wanting   someone tries
to plant a garden   bearded iris
chives wild sweet pea twines
beside imported cream roses

My father loved my mother's
flowers   asked their names
forgetting each even
as she spoke them

Sweet William   Zinnia
   Dusty Miller

I recite them to remember

o

The reach runs deep
between two bays
   cut by a glacier
that scraped out inlets
and peninsulas   necks   harbors
a twine of tributaries
and falls that reverse!

rills and runnels that fill
empty and fill again

Such abundance of coast
pillowed in granite   all
crumpled in against itself

   if one could tug each
end and straighten
 that snaking rope
of intricate seaboard

      where land rises and kneels
      like memory meeting its grave
and where sea finds
meaning in its own absence

   how very long that shore
would be—

            a kind of truth
one can only attempt
to reconstruct   to dream
somehow into being

Cove

I go down the steep path   slick
with   pine needles   my bare toes
grip   roots   soles land hard on
acorn knobs   here and there a
cushion of moss   finally   the
ledge   from   which   to launch
the   tide   flowing   out or in
it must be   brimming   or nearly
to cover   the rocks   there is
no easing into the cold   a gasp
and   I begin   arms and legs
buoyant   take me   toward   the
place   where   the sun touches
down   I tread in its extravagant
colors   the sedge on the shore
bends in wind   light fluent   on
fluent blades   a squall of midges
hovers in air   one song sparrow
tsip tsip   an   osprey   soars
whistling   its   shadow   slips
over   me   as I feel   my   way
through the keen wheeling current

Notes

Duino Elegies, by Rainer Marie Rilke, translated by Stephen Mitchell, 1992.

"Big, with Rift" is an outdoor art installation by Steven Siegel at DeCordova Museum in Lexington, Massachusetts.

"Killdeer" references the Treaty of Saginaw, also known as the Treaty with the Chippewa, on September 24, 1819; more than six million acres were ceded. Indian Dave Stocker, son of Chief Nipmup of the Chippawa, was a well-known figure in Tuscola County, Michigan, and mentioned in several newspaper accounts; he died in 1909 and was believed to have lived 106 years.

"Transit" includes a line from José Saramago's story, "The Chair," in the book, *The Lives of Things*, translated into English by Giovanni Pontiero, Verso Press, 2012.

"No way but" includes a line from John Donne's poem, "Hymn to God, My God, In Sickness."

The title, "part or particle of God," comes from Ralph Waldo Emerson's poem, "The Transparent Eyeball."

Acknowledgements

Grateful acknowledgment is due to the editors of the following publications in which these poems, some in earlier versions, first appeared:

Anastamos:	Killdeer
Fifth Wednesday:	Dementia Diary #5
Heartwood:	Catastophe
Hollins Critic:	Fishing at the dam after my father's funeral
Ibbetson Street:	At Mt. Auburn Cemetery
Kettle and Wolf:	Dear one
Lost Sparrow Press:	Late March and the River's Numb
Naugatuck River Review:	Dementia Diary #16
Olive Press:	At the bonfire a firefly
On the Seawall:	No way but
Panoply:	*Tenshin-en* / Garden of the Heart of Heaven [as, "Zen Garden at the Museum of Fine Arts"]
Ruminate:	*part or particle of God*
Salamander:	Dementia Diary #14
The Blue Nib:	Along the Fens
The Bookends Review:	Bound
	The Hawthorn Speaks
	Opaque
The Helix:	The Meadow
	Navigating the Reach
Wend:	In Flight Detroit – Boston
	Dying takes every day
	Fetch she said

Thanks to my teachers, Phil Legler, Harold Bond, Susan Donnelly, David Semanki, Afaa Michael Weaver, Marilyn Nelson, Danielle Legros Georges, Bruce Weigl, Martha Collins; and to those who read and helped me with drafts of these poems, Ruth Smullin, Philip Burnham, Ruth Chad, Jack LaVert, Victor Howes, and the poets who met at the Yenching Library, including Ellin Sarot, Carmellite Chamblin, and Thomas DeFreitas. Thanks to Steve Dunn for Norton Island, the gift of a residency, and a vocabulary for the Maine coast. Thanks to my nephew Michael who introduced me to the welcoming village of Karluk on Kodiak Island and to my husband Steve who took the stunning photo of its coast for the cover of this book. Deepest gratitude for the friendship and insights of Hilary Sallick and Linda Haviland Conte, without whose steady encouragement I'd feel lost. Love and thanks always to my family.

MARY BUCHINGER, author of *Roomful of Sparrows* (Finishing Line, 2008; New Women's Voices Series semi-finalist); *Aerialist* (Gold Wake, 2015; shortlisted for the May Swenson Poetry Award, the OSU Press/*The Journal* Wheeler Prize for Poetry, and the Perugia Press Prize); einfühlung/*in feeling* (Main Street Rag, 2018); /*klaʊdz*/ (Lily Poetry Review Books, 2021); *Virology* (Lily Poetry Review Books, 2022); *Navigating the Reach* (Salmon Poetry, 2023); and *There is only the sacred and the desecrated* (Lily Poetry Review Books, forthcoming, Paul Nemser Book Prize, Honorable Mention), has received awards from the New England Poetry Club and the Virginia Poetry Society, a Norton Island Residency, and over a dozen Pushcart Prize and Best of the Net nominations. Her poetry appears in *AGNI*, *Hollins Critic*, *Interim*, *Nimrod*, *PANK*, *phoebe*, *Plume*, *Salt Hill*, *Seneca Review*, *Queen Mob's Teahouse*, and elsewhere. Buchinger serves on the board of the New England Poetry Club and teaches at the Massachusetts College of Pharmacy and Health Sciences in Boston. www.MaryBuchinger.com.

Photo: Stephen Bodwell

salmonpoetry

Cliffs of Moher, County Clare, Ireland

"Publishing the finest Irish and international literature."
Michael D. Higgins, President of Ireland